HOW TO SPEAK

Cat

HOW TO SPEAK CAT

This edition published in 2019
By SJG Publishing, HP22 6NF, UK

Author: MIchael Powell

Cover design: Milestone Creative

Contents design: Double Fish Design Ltd

ISBN: 978-1-911517-45-0

Printed in China

10 9 8 7 6 5 4 3 2 1

HOW TO SPEAK

Understand what your cat is trying to tell you

Contents

A MEETING OF MINDS

BODY SENSE

I'M LISTENING

SEE YOU, FEEL YOU

GROWING TOGETHER

I had been told that the training procedure with cats was difficult. It's not. Mine had me trained in two days.

BILL DANA

Introduction

Wouldn't it be great if we could understand our cats beyond the superficial language of meow? But you can become skilled at observing their subtle behavior, feline facial expressions, tail positions and other body language signs and visual markers, as well as an entire superculture of smells. All you need to do is to watch and listen.

Cats make a huge effort to communicate with us. We aren't imagining an entire conversation; cats are highly intelligent autonomous creatures that are adept at communicating with humans as well as each other.

This book will show you how to be a good listener and a keen feline observer. It will encourage you to be vigilant and attentive to the many ways that your cat interacts with you all the time. As soon as you stop making everything about you and stay quiet - physically and especially verbally - you can be more aware of what she is trying to tell you. This will lead you to better serve her needs and deepen the bond of trust between you, creating a happy household.

There is, incidentally, no way of talking about cats that enables one to come off as a sane person.

DAN GREENBERG

A MEETING OF
Minds

ALL CATS ARE

Unique

They have different personalities, degrees of independence, need for social interaction, levels of confidence and intelligence. But they all need an attentive, responsive and responsible owner to keep them secure, safe, healthy and happy. That's you, by the way, as well as everyone else in your home. It's a big responsibility for sure, but this book doesn't go into the usual detail about the nitty-gritty of cat ownership from choosing the right cat food to buying an engaging hunting toy. Instead, it focuses on observation and communication.

Its primary aim is to help you to understand how your cat interacts with and interprets the world through its senses. Ideally, it will help you to be more aware of the many different ways in which your cat communicates with you and other cats. Not only will you have a fascinating glimpse into her world, but you'll have a better appreciation for how she expresses her needs and wants, so that you can pander to her every whim!

The more you understand how your cat functions and interacts with its multisensory environment, the better you will be able to cater to her needs and live harmoniously with your feline friends. You and you cat may share a home, but you experience it in very different ways. Humans typically rely on their eyesight, hearing, touch and smell, while your cat's experience of the same environment is dominated by smells, sounds and, to a lesser extent, eyesight, which is humbling when you consider that when you stumble to the toilet in near darkness in the middle of the night, your cat can see you perfectly and sight is really only her third favorite sense.

You operate on one physical level, living in your head, which is usually several feet above the floor; your cat's domain extends from the crawlspace beneath the sofa to the top of a dusty old wardrobe, even though you think she dwells mainly around your shins.

It's great to feel that our pets are important members of our family, but that doesn't mean that we should treat them like humans. That doesn't mean they are a lesser priority – they should of course be treated with the same respect, thoughtfulness and sensitivity as you would hope to be shown yourself – but trying to understand them human-centrically is very limited. You must climb a little way into their world.

Breed Characteristics

Having just said that all cats are unique, your cat's breed will influence its character and behavior. Entire books have been written on cat breeds and there isn't the space to discuss them in detail here, but you should definitely learn the key characteristics, special requirements and any possible complications associated with your breed before you bring them home, since even the simplest factors will dictate how you should care for them.

For example, hair length usually determines how and how often your cat needs to be groomed. Most cat breeds make ideal family pets, but some, like the Sphynx, although they are very affectionate, require special care that you should know about in advance.

According to John Alderton, author of *Understanding Your Cat*, 'A cat's breed affects the kind of companionship that it prefers'. In *The Cat Whisperer,* Claire Bessant claims that a researcher in the US 'has recognized two different types of feline character within the groups of kittens she has studied . . . excitable and nervous, and those which are much more relaxed and quiet in their attitude to life and its challenges'.

She discusses a similar pattern in adult cats: 'Current work on the personality of the adult cat . . . points to the likelihood of there being two different and distinct types'. She describes type one as needing 'lots of social contact with both people and other cats and is relaxed in their company'. The second type 'seems only to enjoy the company of one or two members of its human family . . . and often doesn't form bonds with other cats either'.

If you have a type two cat, you will find that the more effort you put into cuddling, nurturing and loving her, the less she'll want to know you. She generally won't initiate contact and visitors usually get the cold shoulder treatment. If you have a cat like this, you can stop blaming yourself for having created an aloof little ingrate. She may have been born that way. Bessant concludes that more research needs to be done to discover the extent to which nature and nurture have produced these two types.

KITTENHOOD AND THE BONDING LANGUAGE
of Touch

The strong bond you form with your cat during kittenhood will form the basis for your future relationship, so it's important to get things right early on. A kitten is intensely affected by her early experiences, so it's vital that you understand and respond positively to her needs so that you can give a secure foundation.

Typically, your kitten will arrive from a breeder at about eight weeks old. Although you will have already missed some of her important formative weeks, you still have a window of about four weeks to imprint positive tactile experiences on your kitten. She basically needs to be picked up and handled, stroked, groomed, played with and loved, so that she learns that physical interaction with humans is safe and fun. If a kitten is deprived of the opportunity to experience this close bonding process during the first twelve weeks of life, she will find it very hard to form emotional attachments later.

Pick your kitten up by putting one hand around her chest and under her front legs and steady her with the other hand as you bring her towards your chest. Support her whole body as you cuddle her; don't leave any legs dangling or she'll feel unsafe and start digging her claws into you to feel more secure. Hold the kitten firmly but gently and put her down the moment she starts to struggle. Children especially must be taught to respect the kitten's boundaries and not to hold her against her will. Young children should be supervised at all times with the kitten to make sure they are being gentle and appropriate.

Most kittens like to play fight using nails and teeth. It's very cute and doesn't hurt your hand at this early stage. Avoid play fighting with your hands and use toys instead, otherwise you will teach the kitten that attacking hands is acceptable behavior. Even if you have no problem with this, your guests will. Also, be aware that if you encourage your kitten to attack your toes by wiggling them under the duvet, when she grows up her relentless pouncing on any duvet movement will become very irritating. It is easier to not teach it, rather than have to unlearn it later. Avoid taunting games generally, as these can easily descend into bullying on your part, which undermines your kitten's confidence.

A quiet Homecoming

When you bring your kitten home for the first time, introduce her to a quiet room where she can retreat for a few days until she finds her bearings. It is important to bring her into a quiet environment, protected from the noisy comings-and-goings of the rest of the household, especially young children and other pets. Leave the door slightly ajar so she can venture further when she's gained the confidence. Don't worry if she hides under a bed or behind a wardrobe. It is good for her to find places where she can hide and feel secure, then she will begin to explore her surroundings once she has established her little fortress of solitude.

Place her litter tray in a secluded corner of the quiet room, with her food and water as far away as possible from the litter tray. Use shallow bowls so she doesn't disturb her sensitive little whiskers.

Keep the house as quiet as possible when she first comes home. Before long you can return to your customary noisy shenanigans but don't be surprised if your kitten avoids all the hustle and bustle.

Cats have very sensitive hearing – you don't have to bark orders at them. They also don't appreciate being addressed in that squeaky style that humans reserve for babies and dogs. Cats demand more decorum. They really can't be doing with noisy fussy greetings. She says hello by sticking her tail in the air and she may utter a meow or two, but anything more animated is just so . . . uncool.

When you call her name (e.g. to call her for dinner time), always use an enthusiastic but mellow tone. If you don't sound welcoming she'll be reluctant to come home, and under no circumstances should you shout or get angry. She won't understand why you are being so aggressive and the only lesson it will teach her is that you're scarily unpredictable.

ESPECIALLY

For You

Did you know that apart from hissing and caterwauling, adult cats rarely vocalize with other cats and that their trademark 'meow' is verbal interaction developed specifically to communicate with humans?

That's mind blowing if you think too hard about it. That means over thousands of years of living side-by-side with us, cats have learned that humans can be manipulated, entertained and enthralled by a repertoire of meows (see pages 80-83). Humans have also learned that cats can be taught to recognize certain human vocalizations, which include a limited vocabulary (see page 116), and they can also interpret our emotional state through our intonation.

So, what does this mean? Well, for starters, it's important to keep reminding yourself that when you talk to your cat and she meows back, there is genuine communication there. You aren't imagining an entire conversation; your cat is a highly intelligent autonomous creature that is so adept at communicating that it uses a special language to interact with humans that its species has developed over millennia.

However, if you want to gain a deeper understanding of how your cat communicates, you need to explore beyond the superficial language of meow (think of it as a user-friendly but narrow operating system for humans) beneath which lie sophisticated codices of feline facial expressions, tail positions, ear positions and other body language signs and visual markers (such as scratching) as well as an entire superculture of smells.

All these communication tools will be discussed in greater detail later so that you can really begin to understand what your cat is thinking and feeling. Humans may have domesticated cats (or vice versa) but they remain wild animals with a bundle of hard-wired instincts, needs, desires, predilections and dis-inclinations, which are revealed and expressed in specific ways. As you become more skilled at observing your cat's subtle behavior, you will deepen the unique bond between you and develop an even greater respect for the incredible creature with whom you have the privilege of sharing your home.

UNIQUE COMMUNICATION BETWEEN Cat and Owner

As well as understanding the repertoire of meows (see pages 80-83), there are certain elements of communication between cats and their humans that are unique to that relationship, although they may appear in modified forms elsewhere.

Your cat can show you her love in myriad ways including kneading, bringing you presents, head-butting (bunting), staring into your eyes and slowly blinking, showing you her belly, gently nibbling your finger, rubbing against your legs, following you around and, of course, purring. However, some love tokens are so special and secret that you might not be able to find anyone else whose cat does the same thing. Keep vigilant and be ultra-attentive to the many ways that your cat interacts with you because cats don't gesture accidentally and all physical contact is loaded with meaning.

We should all be able to find things that our cats do that don't seem to be shared by the general feline population, so they must be little personalized touches that have arisen between two individuals. This can also apply to problems, where the owner reinforces antisocial behavior by making a big deal out of it rather than following the general rule of ignoring unwanted habits and rewarding desirable ones (see page 32).

According to Dr John Bradshaw, a biologist at the University of Bristol and author of Cat Sense, cats sometimes see humans either as huge, rubbish cats or as mother-sub-stitutes, not another species, and so will often treat us accordingly. We're so useless we can't even catch mice, but we are curiously adept at opening tins of cat food. How confusing must that be for a cat?

So, the next time your cat licks behind your ear, she may be telling you to step up your personal hygiene or else she's buttering you up for another plate of tuna.

IT ISN'T ALL
About You

Even though we all have a special bond with our cats, to appreciate the sheer effort that they make to communicate with us we must keep reminding ourselves that it isn't all about us. We can be so caught up in our own desire to connect with our cats that we fill the room with noise and activity to coax our furry friends into a response but then miss that they actually initiated the conversation and have been 'talking' to us already. We were so wrapped up in our own pleasure at seeing them that we failed to observe that our cat made the first move and we ignored the subtleties of her communication.

For example, when your cat walks into the room, she'll be saying hello before you even notice she's there, trotting towards you, with her tail up in the air, her ears pricked, eyes wide and happy. She rubs against your leg to say hello again and lets out a little meow. That's when you notice her, pick her up and start talking at her, rubbing her face and tickling behind her ears, holding her a little too close and then, when she struggles to get free, you put her gently back on the floor and feel rebuffed by her aloofness. But had you stepped back and been a bit more observant, you wouldn't have missed all her earlier 'conversation'. She'd already said hello several times and didn't want a full-on body cuddle, she was keeping it cool and then you went and overreacted, like she'd been missing for a week.

Sometimes there's a huge benefit in staying quiet, physically and especially verbally, so that you can be more aware of what she is trying to tell you. Be a good listener and a keen observer and you'll soon realize that cats communicate with their bodies and meow all the time if you know what to look for. For example, if your cat makes a high-pitched meow while walking in a certain direction and keeps looking back at you, follow her. She's trying to draw your attention to something. When you can understand what she's trying to say, it's a delight for both of you, which deepens the bond of trust and encourages further communication.

Say My Name

The current thinking about how to teach your kitten to recognize her name is to start early and motivate her with food rewards. Actually, as with dogs, there's no need to formally teach your kitten her name, as you will use it so much that she will quickly begin to associate it with herself. What you really want is for her to respond to her name when called and that does seem a trickier ask than with most breeds of dog. Hence the old adage that dogs come when called; cats take a message. However, cats can be trained to come when called, and more reliably than you might think.

It is important to build up positive associations with her name. At first you can simply say her name and give her a treat. You'll use her name a lot when greeting or petting, which will always be a positive bonding experience. Once you are sure that she recognizes her name and associates it with herself, you can work on getting her to respond to it when she's called.

Train her when she's feeling hungry. Say her name and give her a small treat and stroke her head. Repeat a few times, then move a few steps away and call her name and add the word 'come' or 'here'. She should trot over to you for her reward. Keep doing this as you gradually increase the space between you. Spend five minutes doing this every day for a week, just before meal time and it should embed quite easily.

Also call her at random times during the day, either from close by or from another room, and reward her with a treat and a stroke of her head if she responds. Soon you'll be able to phase out the treat and the head stroke will be sufficient reward. Re-introduce the food if you feel she's losing enthusiasm or being inconsistent. Eventually, after a few weeks, she will learn that when she hears her name and the word 'come' or 'here' there is a treat and a stroke waiting for her. What she chooses to do with this information is then down to her breed and her individual whims.

HOW SMART ARE

Cats?

Cats are more difficult to study in scientific behavioral and cognitive experiments than many other animals such as dogs or monkeys, mainly because they are less cooperative and more susceptible to stress. However, they have been tested for many of the standard benchmarks that seem to preoccupy researchers, such as 'object permanence', 'physical causality' and 'quantity discrimination'. But there are still significant areas of their sensory world – such as smell – about which we have comparatively little knowledge.

OBJECT PERMANENCE

This is the ability to know the physical location of an object even when you can't see it. Experiments with a cat toy and a sofa cushion will quickly satisfy any cat owner that cats do have the ability to keep in mind an object when it is out of view, rather than assume that is has ceased to exist. Human babies normally gain this skill before the age of two. Cats have been shown to take this one step further. In an 'invisible displacement test', an experimenter shows a cat food being hidden in a container, which is then placed behind a screen. The experimenter then shows the cat an empty container. Cats in such tests have looked behind the screen, deducing that the food is probably still there (because the container was empty).

PHYSICAL CAUSALITY

The standard test for understanding physical causality involves putting food on the end of various bits of string and then observing whether the subject pulls the correct string. In one experiment, fifteen cats were presented with three set-ups: a single string with food at the other end; two parallel strings only one of which was baited; two strings which crossed once, only one of which was baited. All the cats managed to pull the single string to reach the food but none of them consistently pulled the correct string in the other two scenarios, leading to the conclusion that there was no evidence that the cats understood the function of the strings or their physical causality. That said, all cats seem to understand the psychological causality of wailing for the arrival of their dinner.

QUANTITY DISCRIMINATION

There is limited research here, but cats have been trained to tell the difference between two dots and three dots, proving that they can discriminate between small quantities. In tests, cats have also been offered different quantities of food in discrete numerical combinations and they chose the larger quantities more often than the smaller ones.

Expressing
natural behaviors

Cats make a huge compromise to live with humans, sacrificing freedom of movement, the thrill of the hunt, sharing territory, eating what we choose to give them and scratching in designated places. So when they express natural behaviors such as returning home with a freshly caught headless squirrel, our first reaction is rarely to praise. But it is important to acknowledge that your cat has hunting and other instincts that don't disappear just because she spends most of her life sitting on the sofa with you.

If your cat goes outdoors, she will at some point return home with live prey she has caught. Female cats often do this so they can teach their kittens how to hunt. It may be that your cat sees you in a kitten role, despite the fact that you are the provider who knows how to open tins of cat food. Whatever is going on inside that furry head, you can be sure that presenting you with this most valuable trophy (or leaving it on your pillow or favorite chair) is an act of affection, not a wilful attempt to drive you out of your home and mind. Don't scold because she won't understand that she has done anything wrong and she will be very confused that her kindly gesture has been met with so much negativity. Neither should you heap praise on her because that could reinforce the behavior, although of course it will continue to happen even without encouragement.

You can try to transfer all her hunting instincts onto her toys by engaging her in lots of play, but above all remember that hunting small prey is a natural feline urge that is healthy for her mental and physical wellbeing. Scratching is another natural behavior that should be encouraged, but in the correct places: where you want it to happen, rather than on the furniture. Being a responsible cat owner means accepting these and other natural behaviors but directing them such that you can all live happily together under the same roof without repressing your cat's instincts.

USE POSITIVE

Reinforcement

We all love our cats like members of the family. We love having them around and we want them to be happy, sociable members of our household, but sometimes they drive us crazy. They seem to know instinctively how to make our blood pressure rise to dangerous levels and make us want to scream and shout. This is why it's really important always to remember to use positive reinforcement. We know it makes sense, we know it works, but it's so easy to lose the plot and make a bad situation worse and end up with a confused, scolded cat as well as a frustrated owner on the verge of tears.

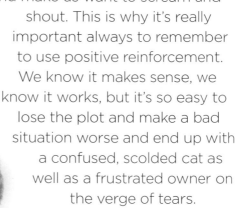

Positive reinforcement is very simple to understand but can be difficult to fully trust. It means ignoring or deterring bad behavior and rewarding desirable behavior. So simple to say, so hard to put into practice when you come home to find your new cushions have been ripped to shreds or there's another dead animal on your pillow. Losing your temper and shouting or punishing is cruel, it never works (especially since the 'naughty' behavior might have happened hours ago) and often it can actually make the problem worse.

It is important to understand what might be causing the unwanted behavior. The answer is often stress and anxiety or your having failed to understand your cat's needs. For example, if you place her litter tray next to a noisy refrigerator or the smelly rubbish bin or in a busy corridor with no privacy, she will show her anxiety by going to the toilet elsewhere, not because she's trying to be naughty but because her needs aren't being met.

When the behavior is unwanted but hasn't been caused by your failure to meet her needs, then you need to use imaginative ways to discourage it. For example, if you don't want the cat to walk on the kitchen worktops, line the edges with foil or double-sided sticky tape. Then when you see your cat avoid the worktop, give her a treat. The reward must come within seconds of the behavior or she may not know what it's for. You also need to reward consistently and make sure everyone in the household does the same. Eventually you'll be able to phase out the food treats and replace them with soothing positive words.

As anyone who has ever been around a cat for any length of time well knows, cats have enormous patience with the limitations of the human kind.

CLEVELAND AMORY

BODY

Sense

BE AWARE OF YOUR OWN

Body Language

Even though your cat has learned that you respond best to verbal interaction, less well to facial expressions (see page 108) and are completely useless at reading smells, she will still respond strongly to your visual cues and read a lot into your body language.

It's important you understand the messages you send to her using your body, many of which you may be completely unaware of.

We've all experienced the moment when a cat walks into a room and ignores all the cat lovers who stare admiringly and makes straight for the person who is afraid of cats, who is sitting quietly on the sofa trying to make himself look as small and uninviting as possible. It doesn't take much cat empathy to understand why this happens. The cat perceives all those staring people as a threat. When cats greet, they don't stare. The cat who is already in the room demonstrates her contentment with the visitor's arrival by looking away, by remaining calm and still, just like the human ailurophobe.

Your sheer physical presence can make a cat feel uncomfortable. When you stand up, you appear like a skyscraper to your tiny cat. If you want to put her at ease, get down on her level. When she meows to try to communicate with you, smile and let her see your face (which she won't be able to read very effectively when your head is way up in the clouds). When you are sitting down, you may need to pick up your cat and place her on or alongside you so that she can be closer to you, otherwise she may be deterred by your size, you big ol' slab of human. That's why sitting down and beckoning by tapping the sofa doesn't always work.

When your cat has been naughty, if you loom over her to tell her off it's little wonder she looks away from you nonchalantly, in seeming defiance. Remember, you're enormous. She's not ignoring you, she's appeasing you. She probably has no idea why you are angry and are raising your voice but looking away is her attempt to minimize conflict. The next time you go off on a rant, bear in mind that ignoring unwanted behavior and rewarding desirable behavior is the best way to live in harmony with your cat, rather than trying to dominate physically and verbally.

BODY LANGUAGE –
Greeting

You can tell a lot more about a cat from its body language than you can by its vocalizations, if you know what to look for. When cats communicate with each other they rely on smell and body language – facial features, body posture, tail position and movement, shape of the pupils, position of the ears and whiskers. All these visual cues express a cat's mood.

The body language of greeting and inclusion is unmistakable and proves that cats aren't loners. Greeting cats approach each other with their tails up, trotting forward. When they meet, they exchange scents by rubbing their necks, bodies and tails against each other.

When your cat greets you with her tail up, she will also look at your face and may place her paws up your legs so she can get closer to your face. She may also make a greeting trill sound (see page 86). You know when you're being greeted – those leg rubs are hard to ignore – but when you see that tail stick straight up, it is important that you register that your cat is pleased to see you. Reciprocate by rubbing your cat's neck or getting down on the floor so she can see your face and rub scent into your neck.

A perfunctory 'hello' followed by grunts of irritation as she weaves in and out of your legs, just won't crack it as a satisfactory greeting. In fact, it's plain rude.

When you return home, or even if your cat wanders into a room and then pops her tail in the air, it is important that you acknowledge her. She's pleased to see you so don't snub her greeting. Give her your full attention and consciously return the greeting verbally and physically. The more effort you make to fully engage in these special moments, the deeper the bond of trust that will grow between you. These social interactions are a vital way of strengthening the bonds between your cat and the other members of the household too. Every time you greet, you reaffirm group membership.

Cats never stint on this wonderful ritualized behavior. We humans could do well to learn from them and make sure that we greet all the humans in our household in a fully present way. Too often we shout a greeting as we run upstairs, or grunt as we slump on the sofa, and many parents are used to being completely ignored by teenage children until an hour after they arrive.

BODY LANGUAGE –
Relaxed and Happy

Lying or sitting with her ears up and facing forwards, whiskers hanging down her face, front feet folded in the direction of her body. Tail curled up alongside the body. Eyes sleepy looking, maybe partially closed, with pupils oval in shape. You may hear her purring and she may curl into a ball and fall asleep, or stretch out and lie on her back, exposing her belly. This is the ultimate sign of relaxation and trust, but it isn't necessarily an invitation for you to start rubbing her belly.

She looks so cute that you can't resist, but don't be surprised if she tolerates a couple of strokes and then gets her back legs ready for a scratch. Remember, when she stretches and rolls around on her back, it isn't all about you. Have you thought how irritating it must be for a cat that every time they settle down and are just getting comfortable, along comes a human and starts rubbing in their most vulnerable place? Spare a thought for your cat's blissful state, rather than always looking to satisfy your urge to scrunch, cuddle and stroke, no matter how adorable and inviting she looks.

The degree to which your cat is curled up is also an indicator of her temperature.

Cats are very sensitive to heat as they have no sweat glands, so they must adjust their body position to stay warm. At temperatures of 70°F or more, there is very little curl. The tail is curled around a fairly straight body, with the paws in front. As the temperature cools, your cat will incline her head and tuck it into her body and draw her feet in underneath her body, until at a temperature of 55°F, half her face will be covered by her tail and her feet are no longer visible.

If she's happy after walking into the room and greeting you, she may do something else, unique to her, to attract your attention. For example, she might tread on your foot with her back foot and then press it a few times. That's her equivalent of giving you a little hug. Be attentive to these idiosyncrasies, which will be unique with each of your cats. Cats don't gesture accidentally and all physical contact is loaded with meaning.

BODY LANGUAGE –
Anxious and Stressed

When a cat feels anxious, she keeps her head and body low, moves her ears around nervously to listen for threats (or else flattens her ears against her head) and draws back her whiskers along the sides of her face. The tail is carried low, touching the floor.

She will maintain this position while she quietly assesses the threat. At this stage she is making herself as small as possible to appear less threatening. If she is cornered or feels that she needs to become more assertive, she will switch to defensive anger and make herself appear bigger (see page 45).

Her eyes will be open and unblinking and her pupils dilated into an oval or circle. As her anxiety increases, she might start to cower and look really abject and miserable. The tail might be still or moving slowly side to side at the tip.

If you see your cat displaying this body language, offer her verbal and physical reassurance and see if you can locate the source of her anxiety. There may be a stranger outside (or inside) the house. Like humans, cats can get stressed for many reasons, but change is the most common reason. What in her immediate environment has changed?

You may be able to distract her with some play, which will help take her mind off the perceived threat and work out some of that adrenaline. Put on some soothing music or reduce the level of noise in the house if necessary (is the television blaring or are children screaming?). If the anxiety persists, you might use a pheromone diffuser, a simple device which sprays calming hormones into the air, to signal that all is well.

Other signs of persistent anxiety include urinating outside the litter box, diarrhoea, constipation or other digestive issues, excessive grooming or scratching, excessive hiding, increased vocalization, a decrease in appetite and excessive sleeping. Consult your vet to try to figure out what's wrong.

As her immediate anxiety reduces you will observe her body relax and return to the neutral state. The ears will appear perkier and the whiskers will stick out rather than being stuck to her face. She may yawn and stretch and then groom herself to help calm herself down.

BODY LANGUAGE –
Anger And Fear

When a cat is scared or angry its body language presents the same, because both are a response to a perceived threat. The body language of extreme fear is expressed as defensive aggression, designed to prevent but prepare for what neither cat wants – a full on physical fight.

As explained on page 42, an anxious cat keeps her head and body low, moves her ears around nervously to listen for threats (or else flattens her ears against her head), draws back her whiskers along the sides of her face and carries her tail low, touching the floor. A defensive cat will often hold its head to the side and make darting sidelong glances rather than look directly at the aggressor. If she is cornered or feels that she needs to become more assertive, she will switch to defensive anger and make herself appear bigger.

To make herself look as big as possible, she will stand tall, trying to intimidate the other cat with her size. Some cats straighten their front legs to appear taller or arch their backs and fluff themselves up. Her ears are flattened and turned away so that the soft fleshy front is protected in case of attack. By now the whiskers are raised and so is the fur along the cat's back, all to increase her size. This display is to deter the opponent and prevent a physical fight. At this stage you'll also hear some vocalizations (see page 88).

She may also turn partly sideways towards the opponent, which gives her the option of fleeing or fighting. She will also position herself so that she has an escape route. Eyes will be open very wide, with pupils fully dilated. By now the tail may be slashing vigorously from side to side.

As the anger increases, the cat becomes more rigid, with the tail held out stiff. An aggressive cat will hold its head low with its eyes firmly fixed upon its mark (the assertive stare). Eyes are hard and focused and the pupils may narrow, although some angry cats maintain their round, unblinking eyes. Ears are turned fully away and flattened to the head.

BODY LANGUAGE –

Focused

Watch her snap into focused body language when you dangle her favorite toy or get out the catnip, or if she wants something from you, like food. Then her tail will stick up vertically like an exclamation mark. If she's in focused hunting or play-hunting mode, the tail will be kept low and behind the body, maybe quivering slightly at the tip.

Her pupils are open wide with pupils narrowed. Her ears and whiskers will be pricked with friendly curiosity and facing forward, and her body will be angled towards the focus of her attention. If she's stalking a toy (or real prey) she will keep her body low to the ground, with her hind legs coiled under her body, ready to pounce. Her tail will start to twitch as she readies herself to pounce.

If you (or what you can give her – maybe a tin of tuna) are the object of her intense focus, then you can expect lots of scenting ankle rubs as she weaves smoothly between your legs and she might get quite vocal (see page 81). Generally though, in this state she will keep her mouth closed, lips relaxed.

Don't ignore her when she's in a focused playful mood. It's a great compliment that she wishes to initiate play and it's a great way for you to bond while she expends some energy. If you ignore her, she may steal things or invade your personal body space (e.g. by climbing onto your laptop) to attract your attention, especially if you reinforce this behavior by scolding her. Even negative attention is better than no attention at all.

She may steal objects because of her predatory instinct and because she's looking for environmental stimulation as well as different textures to bite and chew. Your cat may also steal because she is anxious and taking objects helps to relieve the stress. So even if you don't mind your knick-knacks disappearing, pay close attention to your cat's wellbeing and be prepared to give her more attention and a variety of stimulation, or help to calm her anxiety, as you feel is appropriate in the circumstances.

BODY LANGUAGE –
Frustrated

Frustration is really just another word for stress. It is caused by the inability to satisfy a need or desire and it can be the root cause of much so-called 'problem behavior'. If your cat appears grumpy, has unpredictable moods and behavior (such as lashing out during what you thought was a nice relaxing stroking session), is scratching or urinating in the 'wrong' place or keeps being wilfully 'naughty' (in defiance of your best training efforts) you have a frustrated cat. All these behaviors are a signal that one or more of her needs or desires are not being met. It's your job to figure out what is lacking.

Despite their reputation as prima donnas, cats need very little to be happy and secure. They like routine, need their own space/territory where they can feel safe, good food and water, something good to scratch (in the right place), regular playtimes (at least twice a day), toys to play with and a clean litter tray. Can you think of anything else? OK, plenty of love and cuddles when they're in the mood, but you're probably providing those already in spades.

An actively frustrated cat usually focuses intently on their object of frustration, so that will give you clues about what they want! They may pace impatiently if they can't get to what they want. A frustrated cat won't rest or settle near you and won't get comfortable. All her senses are honed in on what she wants – eyes will be wide open with pupils dilated, ears forward and whiskers forward-pointing and spread. Try to figure out what's bugging her because if you fail to meet her needs over a prolonged period (days and weeks), her frustration can grow into depression, she may lose her appetite, become lethargic and withdrawn.

Always come back to the basics listed above. Cats make a huge compromise to live with humans, so if you're not maintaining your side of the agreement/social contract, your cat has every right to vent her frustration.

TAIL
Talk

A cat's tail is one of the most expressive parts of its body and it can send messages over quite long distances because it's so big and impossible to ignore.

- Tail at 20 degrees from vertical. Relaxed.

- Tail curved over back. Happy, friendly.

- Tail up. Friendly greeting, invitation to play.

- Tail up, hooked at end. Friendly greeting with some uncertainty.

- Tail up and quivering. Very pleased to see you.

- Pushed straight down. Potentially aggressive.

- Tip flicking. Minor irritation.

- Flicking side to side. Major irritation.

- Tail arched and down. Aggressive.

- Tail arched and fluffed up. Ready for a confrontation; combined with arched back, making himself look bigger and more threatening.

Eyesight

Sighted humans are driven by what they see and it's their primary way of interpreting the world around them. It's easy to forget that a cat's eyesight is less important than smell and hearing, except when hunting. Also, a cat's eye differs greatly from ours in its design and performance. When communicating with your cat using your sight, bear these differences in mind because your cat doesn't see the world in quite the same way as you.

The retina, the light sensitive area inside the eye, is composed of two types of photoreceptors: cones and rods. The cones allow color vision and high visual acuity (i.e. seeing in detail), while the rods operate at lower light levels but with a lower visual acuity. Cats have about one fifth of the visual acuity of humans, so when she stares at your big goofy smiling face from across the room, she doesn't see what you see when you look in the mirror. Your face will look blurry until you get a bit closer – her vision is sharpest when you're about two or three feet apart.

In cats' eyes there are about 25 rods to each cone. Human eyes have four rods to one cone. Cats only need about one sixth of the light we need to see, which is why they can hunt so effectively in near darkness (although they can't actually see in the dark).

The light-sensitive layer at the back of the eyeball is called the retina; behind this is a special reflective layer called the tapetum lucidum, which reflects light back onto the retina, improving low light vision even further (it's also the reason cats' eyes glow in the dark). The pupil also differs from ours. It can open and close more quickly, so it can adjust to light changes more rapidly. It becomes slit shaped in bright light, wide open and circular in dim light. Cats have better peripheral vision than humans (about 205 degrees to our 180) but we see better in color. Cats aren't color blind. They can distinguish between blues and greens, but reds not so well.

EYE
Communication

Cats have large expressive eyes; it's one of the reasons we find them so cute and irresistible. But look more closely and you can read your cat's emotional state.

PUPIL CLUES

The shape of the pupils correspond to your cat's mood. Narrow slits can indicate irritation and anger (or it might just be sitting in bright sunlight!). Wide pupils can indicate alertness: fear or excitement. Watch those pupils open wide when you dangle her favorite toy or get out the catnip. When she's relaxed, she'll have droopy, sleepy-looking eyelids and might even throw you a kitty eye blink kiss.

SLOW EYE BLINKS

Eye contact is really important for human interaction. Generally, in Western human culture, the more we like someone or something, the more we stare. Making good eye contact is a sign of trustworthiness and confidence and shows that we are paying attention to the other person.

The more comfortable we are in someone's presence, the greater the eye contact. Couples in love stare deeply into each other's eyes. Staring lovingly at your cat may feel like the most natural way to express your affection. Unfortunately, your cat doesn't see the world in the same way as you. When she sees you eyeballing her, she thinks 'What are you lookin' at?' and assumes you're thinking the same.

It's important to remind yourself that cats use eye contact differently to humans. A cat will stare intently at something that holds strong interest such as its prey or a perceived threat. It also uses its extensive peripheral vision to constantly monitor its environment, making it especially alert to sudden movement.

Cats are territorial, so when two of them stare at each other it is usually confrontational. They use their unblinking stare to warn off other felines to avoid a fight. We've all seen two cats stare each other down before the dominant cat chases the other one away (or there's a scrap).

When cats want to use their eyes to express trust and affection, they perform slow, languid blinks. By blinking slowly in your cat's presence, you indicate that you pose no threat and that you trust her not to attack you while your eyes are closed! But pick your moment. If your cat responds with wide-eyed fear (or more likely, indifference), wait until she's more in the mood.

Hearing

Cats have incredible hearing that is much better than ours. We can only hear up to about 20kHz, but a cat can hear up to 60kHz. In fact, she will usually detect the high-pitched squeak of her rodent prey before she sees it, while we remain aurally oblivious.

A cat can locate her prey very accurately just using sound. In fact, if you were to observe a blind cat playing with a mouse toy on the ground, you wouldn't be able to tell she was blind, so well could she track its movements using sound and vibrations (detected by her whiskers).

Cats respond well to toys or objects that make high-pitched sounds, like crinkled cellophane, because it mimics to some extent the sound of its prey. Equally, some ordinary household objects freak cats out because of their acute hearing. For example, a sheet of tin foil makes lots of high-frequency noise and probably sounds quite jarring to an ultrasonic feline ear.

Cats' ears are very mobile. They can turn independently through 180 degrees of motion, so the cat can collect sound without moving her head. Even when she is apparently relaxing, notice how her ears keeping moving, alert to possible dangers or prey opportunities.

Cats have thirty muscles to move each ear, while humans have six. So when she doesn't respond to your call, you can be sure she hears you and is choosing to ignore your pesky whining. You aren't paranoid, sometimes she really does wish you'd leave her alone.

Other high-pitched sounds that cats respond well to are the plaintive squeaking of a kitten and the territorial caterwauling of other cats – so much of your cat's auditory experience takes place in this higher end of the auditory spectrum. She might come running for her dinner when she smells it, but more likely because she hears the sound of a tin being opened, or even the familiar noise of a squeaky hinge on the door of the cat food cupboard. Bear this in mind when you want to understand how cats experience the sounds around them or if you want to attract their attention with noises.

Cats are also sensitive to differences in pitch. Scientists have discovered that cats can distinguish between half tones on the musical scale. This skill is important in order to discern different types of prey.

EAR

Position

Cats communicate with their ears. Their ear position and shape changes with the cat's mood and circumstances. A happy, relaxed cat has ears facing forward and tilted back slightly. If it is suddenly roused by a sight, smell or sound, the cat's ears prick up and may begin to twitch and swivel if the cat is uncertain, trying hard to pick up data.

As the cat becomes more agitated the ears move back and flatten against the head. If you can see the inside of the cat's ear, all is well. If the cat is staring at you face on and its ears are swivelled so that the insides are pointing backwards, she is about to attack or is preparing to be attacked. The soft fleshy inner ear is turned away from the threat. At the moment of attack, the ear is flicked down flat against the head for maximum protection.

Some breeds of cat (such as the Maine Coon) have tufts of hair on their ear tips to accentuate this important visual ear language so it can be seen at a greater distance. Physical conflict is always a last resort and resolving territorial disputes at a distance is always preferable.

Whiskers

Take a moment to discover your cat's whiskers. There are about a dozen on either side of her face on the upper lip, above the eyes and on the chin. Cats also have coarse hairs on their elbows which help to form a multimedia sensory picture.

This network of whiskers is extremely sensitive but it works in quite a simple way. Whiskers grow from deeper in the skin than normal hairs, so when they move, the leverage generated at their base creates a strong signal for the nerve cells, which then send messages to the cat's brain to the same area responsible for interpreting information from the eyes. The brain uses both sets of data to create a detailed map of the environment.

When a cat is relaxed and happy it shows in her whiskers, which splay out in a natural fan pointing downwards. An alert, excited or angry cat often pushes her whiskers out to the side ('jazz hands') and forward. When she's under threat, she draws her whiskers along the sides of her face.

Whiskers are highly mobile. Cats move their whiskers forward when hunting, helping them to sense their prey at close range. Cats also have a reflex which makes their eyes narrow or close when it feels a touch on its whisker. This provides important protection when she's prowling around the undergrowth, fixated on her prey, and stops her being smacked in the eye by grass and twigs.

If you want to stay on friendly terms with your cat, don't play with its whiskers. Just leave them alone, no matter how tempting they are to flick, tweak and pull. Also, be especially vigilant around children as they can't resist messing with them. It is very uncomfortable for your cat, no matter how affectionately you fiddle.

Yes, it is cute how she closes her eyes every time you flick her whiskers, but it makes you the worst kind of pet owner. One of the first things to learn about cats, or indeed any pet, is to avoid interacting with them in a way that gives you pleasure at their expense. You may think you're doing no harm but making your pet the butt of your joke is deeply unhealthy and a very worrying trait in a human being.

Mouth

Dogs and human babies love to use their mouths to explore their world; cats not so much (except for when they smell with their mouth open, which is called flehmening – see page 66). However, you can learn a little about your cat's mood by looking at its mouth. For example, like humans, cats yawn for a variety of reasons – when they are relaxed and content, when they want to stay alert, when they want to signal relaxation to other cats, or simply when they are bored.

Yawning expels carbon dioxide and increases oxygen intake, thus helping to increase alertness. A sleepy cat will stretch and yawn immediately upon waking, to ready its mind and body for activity. However, if you stroke your sleeping cat you may elicit a yawn as a gentle warning asking you to back off and leave her alone. A yawn can also be a nervous reaction, an involuntary act of self-calming during times of stress. Cats will certainly groom themselves when they are feeling stressed and sometimes a yawn may form part of this procedure; it all depends on the context. A contented yawn involves closing of the eyes, whereas the eyes remain open during a nervous or calming yawn.

When a cat licks her lips it can be a sign of anxiety (unless you are opening a tin of tuna at the time – once again, context is important). Conversely, if she sits with her tongue lolling out, she is content and relaxed. It is normal for her tongue to poke out of her mouth during sleep.

Sometimes a cat will dart its tongue in and out when trying to remove something unsavoury from its mouth or something stuck on the barbs on its tongue. If this lasts for more than a few minutes, check inside the cat's mouth for injuries or obstructions. If her tongue repeatedly hangs out accompanied by drooling, this could be a sign of periodontal disease or a chipped tooth, so consult a vet. If it's a hot day, your cat may stick her tongue out to regulate her temperature (ineffectively) – make sure she has access to shade and plenty of fresh water.

Cats sometimes show displeasure or disgust by opening the mouth slightly with the nose barely wrinkled. They will also gently ward off other cats by drawing the lips back and swinging the head from side to side.

NOSE AND SENSE
of Smell

The nose is the cat's most important sense organ. Cats have around 200 million smell-receptors in the olfactory epithelium, twice as many as humans have, making their sense of smell much more acute. They also have a special scent organ in the roof of their mouths called the vomeronasal (or Jacobson's) organ (see page 66).

Cats are born blind and deaf, so their sense of smell is vital for their survival long before they use it to track their prey. Kittens don't respond to auditory stimuli until they're 11-16 days old and visual stimuli until they're 16-21 days old. Newborns use smell to locate their mother's nipple and will even return to the same one to feed. The mother knows her kittens by their scent and by rubbing her own scent on them. Exchanging smells is a primary method of communication among cats and between cats and their owners, which is why they like to rub themselves against you (see page 70).

Cats have comparatively few taste receptors on the tongue, so their sense of smell is the stimulant for their appetite. That's the main reason why cats stop eating when they have a respiratory or nasal infection. If they can't smell it, they won't eat it.

Each cat has a unique smell, like a fingerprint. They mark their territory by rubbing, scratching (see page 72), spraying urine (see page 74) and sometimes with their faeces (although they usually bury it). A cat can tell precisely who has been in the neighborhood and how long ago just by using these scent markers. She can also smell whether food is edible or toxic.

Did you know that the color of your cat's nose is related to the color of her fur? Black cats have black noses, white cats have pink noses, orange cats have orange noses, grey cats have grey noses and multicolored cats can have mottled noses. The ridges and markings on a cat's nose are unique, like a fingerprint.

A healthy cat's nose should be cool and moist, but a dry nose isn't necessarily a cause for concern. Some happy healthy cats have dry noses, so it's only a bad sign when accompanied by other clues of illness such as lethargy, loss of appetite and a high temperature (good luck using that rectal thermometer). Conversely, a runny nose may be a sign of an upper respiratory infection – if in doubt, contact your vet.

THE FLEHMEN

Reaction

As if cats didn't already have an amazing sense of smell, they can also perform a nifty manoeuvre that enables them to combine taste and smell in a thin tube of cartilage called the vomeronasal organ, or Jacobson's organ, located in the roof of the mouth behind the front teeth. The Flehmen Reaction sounds like the title of a Robert Ludlum novel but is actually an awesome dating app located inside your cat's skull!

Cats can learn heaps of information about other cats in the neighborhood using the Flehmen Reaction. It's an important tool for communication and receiving messages from other cats, in which unfortunately we humans can play no part. We can only be ignorant bystanders, watching jealously while our kitty decodes the pheromones in the air to determine the age, sex and reproductive status of the local feline scene.

The word originates from the German 'flehmen', meaning to bare the upper teeth, and also from the Upper Saxon German flemmen, 'to look spiteful'. Jacobson's organ is named after the nineteenth century Danish surgeon who was fascinated by the human vomeronasal organ (which modern scientists believe has sadly limited function).

You can tell when your cat is 'doing a flehmen' because she will stop, raise her head, open her mouth and then curl up her top lip in a grimace to reveal her teeth and gums. She presses her tongue against the roof of her mouth, which transfers the smell chemicals into the Jacobson's organ, allowing her to kind of taste the smell. She may hold this position for several seconds without it affecting her regular breathing – she can continue to breathe while keeping the chemical cloud trapped inside her head.

It does look a bit trippy, but don't be alarmed. About half of domestic cats respond to catnip in this way. Toms use the Flehmen Reaction more frequently than female cats, but it is common in both sexes and is also performed by wild cats such as lions and tigers. It has been observed in a wide range of species such as horses, zebras, giraffes, goats, elks, snakes, giant pandas and even hedgehogs.

TOUCHING NOSES AND BUMPING *Foreheads*

Cats often greet by rubbing against each other to mingle scents (see page 70). Touching noses (sometimes called 'sniffing noses') and bumping foreheads are delightfully cute extensions of this behavior.

Nose touching is one of the first social interactions learned during kittenhood. Born blind and deaf, the sense of smell and the touch receptors on the nose are in full working order, so nose touching is how kittens make early contact with their mother and their litter mates. The nose and lips are also sensitive to temperature and are important for locating the mother's nipple and seeking out warmth. Once learned, this nose touching interaction is never forgotten and continues to be used throughout the cat's life.

Nose touching and forehead bumping not only allow cats to smell each other and exchange scents, but they are also expressions of hierarchy and trust, since putting the face close to the mouth and teeth of another cat leaves both parties vulnerable.

You can greet a cat with a nose touch, using your finger as a nose if it's a strange cat, or your own nose if you trust that your cat is comfortable and familiar with nose touching with you. With a strange cat, sit or crouch down to the cat's level and then gently extend your arm, offering your curled index finger for the cat to sniff and nose touch. Make sure your arm approaches from the front rather than from above, which can feel threatening. If the cat feels relaxed enough to head bunt you (see below), show your appreciation by gently rubbing their chin while talking sweetly.

Cats also show affection by bumping foreheads or by bumping their heads against any available part of your body, such as your leg. This is known as head bunting. Scent glands above the eye, but below the ear, secrete scent on you so that you all smell the same. When there are several cats in a household, the dominant cat initiates the head bunting and takes on the responsibility of making sure that the common feline scent is spread amongst every member of the household, including the humans and often the dog too.

Rubbing

Cats have special scent glands under their chins, at the corners of the mouth, on either side of the forehead, at the base of their tail and in between the toes. These glands release a unique and highly detailed chemical marker which indicate status, mark territory and even advertise sexual availability. Cats who live in groups often rub against each other in greeting.

While it is true that cats like to rub their signature smell on just about everything in the house – furniture, door frames, curtains, humans, discarded clothing and other animals, they do prioritize certain areas that they will return to again and again, such as entrances to the home or nesting places, areas of high animal traffic as well as territorial boundaries. The territorial scent markers are especially important as they can prevent physical fights over territory, which are always the last resort.

Never forget that if you are a cat owner, you and your

home are literally drenched in cat pheromones – the scent equivalent of pages and pages of your cat's Tinder profile. A cynical explanation of what is happening when your cat rubs against you is that she isn't showing affection but is instead 'claiming you as her property'. This isn't strictly true. She's claiming everything as hers and vice versa – she wants everyone to mingle their scents so that they belong to the same tribe. She's spreading the collective ownership as well as the love!

Now, if she were to use you as a scratching post, you should be rightfully worried and a little bit insulted, since she is using you as nothing more than a territorial marker – a furniture leg – rather than signalling that you're a member of her big happy family.

If a strange cat rubs against you in greeting, it isn't necessarily a sign of affection. She is leaving her scent and investigating yours. She's checking you out, rather than inviting you to tickle her chin, and it is certainly not an invitation for you to start e n e r g e t i c a l l y stroking her back. If you crassly misinterpret her approaches, don't be surprised when she scoots away with a flea in her ear.

Scratching

Domestic cats sharpen their claws by scratching, using either the bark of a tree, a designated scratching post, or worst-case scenario – assorted furniture, curtains and upholstery. However, scratching also has an important role in communication and if your cat is scratching in the wrong places and destroying your soft furnishings, she is actually sending a powerful territorial message. Don't forget that all scratching is visual and olfactory marking – it's yet another form of cat speak.

Domestic cats routinely begin to mark their scent in the home more frequently if another cat has been introduced into the household. The visible claw marks and the scent deposited by scent glands between the toes as well as sweat glands on the paw pads, are territorial markers for the explicit attention of the feline interloper. Your cat isn't trying to take its revenge on you – get over yourself, you are not her intended audience. As soon as you recognize that scratching is one of the ways cats speak, you're well on your way to solving any scratching issues.

Even if you haven't introduced a new kitty, if your cat is scratching in inappropriate places, place a commercial scratching post next to the unwanted spot and make it more enticing by rubbing in a few drops of essential oil of valerian. If possible, try to repair or cover over the visible scratches on the furniture so she doesn't keep getting the same visual cues to repeat the vandalism.

If you have multiple cats in your household, you may be lucky enough that they are content to share one scratching post, but you will more than likely need to invest in several, ideally one for each cat, just as you should provide a separate litter tray for each animal. As well as the possible territorial anxiety caused by sharing posts, cats often have individual preferences, some prefer vertical areas while others favour horizontal scratching, as well as different textures.

You're dead right cats are fussy and it's your job to make sure that their environment is near perfect, otherwise everyone will end up miserable.

Spraying

Cats spray by backing up against a vertical surface with tail erect and squirting a small amount of urine. It's the same as regular urine but it differs from normal urinating by its position and quantity. Cats do regular urinating by squatting down on a horizontal surface and the quantity of urine is greater.

The majority of cats that spray are unneutered males. Most start spraying around 6 to 7 months of age, so vets advise neutering at 6 months of age as your cat reaches maturity. If your cat is spraying around the house, he is marking his territory.

He's not talking directly to you, but he is showing stress and communicating to other cats and you can infer from this behavior that he feels under threat. He's not trying to annoy you, he's not sulking at you and he doesn't deserve to be punished. If you want the spraying to stop (and if you've smelled cat urine, you will want it to stop) it's your responsibility to make your cat feel more secure.

First, clean the spraying area with an enzymatic cleaner or vinegar to eliminate the scent, otherwise he will keep spraying in the same place. Avoid using cleaners that contain ammonia; this may encourage further spraying because ammonia is present in urine.

You can place citrus peels around your garden to discourage other cats from entering. Spray your entrances with commercial cat repellent that contains citrus oil. If you think the spraying has been caused by the introduction of new pets into the household or because your cat's environment has changed in some way, the spraying should stop in time as your cat becomes more settled, as long as you scrupulously clean existing spray areas. You can also use positive reinforcement to help your cat associate the spray area (a place of anxiety) with happier events such as feeding, playing with a toy or having a cuddle.

If you think your cat is urinating rather than spraying, there may be an issue with sharing a litter tray (one each), its placement (lacking privacy) or its lack of cleanliness. There are also medical reasons for inappropriate urinating, such as urinary tract problems, diabetes, arthritis or kidney failure. If in doubt, get your cat checked out at the vet.

Kneading

You've probably experienced it dozens of times – your cat jumps up on your lap or lies on your chest, then starts stomping on you, alternating rhythmically with her front paws like you're a big pile of grapes that urgently need squishing. Some cats even use all four paws. If she uses her claws, even though you're feeling discomfort, she's in seventh heaven in an almost trancelike state. Believe it or not, kneading is yet another form of cat communication, combining self-soothing with territorial marking.

One reason why cats knead is related to kittenhood, when the kitten kneads the mother's belly while nursing, stimulating the let-down response so that the mother's milk flows. The kitten feels secure and is rewarded with milk. Cats carry the association of kneading with pleasure and relaxation well into adulthood. Some people believe it's a sign that the cat has been weaned too early, but the practise is so widespread that this is unlikely. Young children gain comfort by sucking their thumb or a soother, regardless of whether they have been weaned, because its a pleasurable activity.

However, there is another motivation behind the kneading. Cats have scent glands between their toes near the base of the claws. We humans can't detect the scent, but the surface the cat kneads becomes impregnated with their unique smell, which then sends a smell message to other cats that this is reserved territory. She might even try to leave a few signature scratches as a visual clue, like she does on her scratching post, all of which sends the message 'This is my nice warm lap – keep off'.

If your unneutered female cat makes plaintive meows while she is kneading, it could be a sign that she's going into heat. She may also pace restlessly and spray. Sometimes cats knead simply to tell their human companions that they want some attention. If your cat spends a lot of time kneading you, don't fret about whether she was weaned too young, just enjoy the moment knowing that she is feeling very secure, content and comfortable.

The way to get on
with a cat is to treat it
as an equal – or even better,
as the superior it knows
itself to be.

ELIZABETH PETERS

I'M

Listening

Moelk's Sixteen Meows

In 1944, New York psychologist Mildred Moelk discovered that cats meow differently to people than to fellow cats. She categorized 16 sounds used in cat-human and cat-cat communication, which are still applicable today for understanding feline vocalizations. They first appeared in her paper 'Vocalizing in the House Cat: A Phonetic and Functional Study' in the April 1944 Journal of Comparative Psychology.

Moelk also showed that cats frequently vary the duration, intensity, tone, pitch, roughness, stress and speed of the sound and also use repetition to get their message across. However, animal behaviorists have more recently suggested that these sounds aren't as nuanced as Moelk would have us believe. Since the cat's main goal is to attract human attention, it soon learns that if it complains with sufficient intensity, pitch and nauseating repetition, humans will do anything to shut it up! As you will already know first hand, a cat's meows can range from a gentle coaxing request to a full throttle incessant and indignant command.

Moelk organized the vocalizations into three patterns based on how cats formed the sounds:

1. Murmur Patterns: consonant made with mouth closed, breath passes through the nose
2. Vowel Patterns: breath passes through the open mouth as it closes
3. Strained Intensity Patterns: voiced breath forced through the mouth which is held wide open.

An apostrophe (') means an emphasis, most often from inhalation, and a long dash (––) is a sustained sound.

MURMUR PATTERNS: express greeting or satisfaction, eg 'hello', 'pay attention to me'

1. Purr ('hrn-rhn-'hrn-rhn)
2. Request or Greeting ('mhrn'hr'hrn)
3. Call ('mhrn)
4. Acknowledgment or Confirmation ('mhng)

VOWEL PATTERNS: requests or complaints, eg 'give me', 'please give me'

1. Demand ('mhrn-a'––ou)
2. Begging Demand ('mhrn-a––ou––)
3. Bewilderment ('maou?)
4. Complaint ('mhng-a––ou)
5. Mating Cry – mild form ('mhrn-a––ou)
6. Anger Wail (wa––ou––)

STRAINED INTENSITY PATTERNS: arousal or stress, eg 'I like' or 'I don't like'

1. Growl (grrrrr)
2. Snarl (aye-a)
3. Mating Cry (ooy-ooy-a)
4. Pain Scream (aye-ee)
5. Refusal Rasp (aye-aye-aye)
6. Spitting (fff-tu)

A REPERTOIRE OF

Meows

Cats really do have a repertoire of meows, something for every occasion. You will know better than anyone what your cat's meows mean. Be heartened that you are not imagining this interaction or merely anthropomorphising your feline friends. Your cat has learned from experience (some would argue, the experience of training you to do her bidding) that vocalizations get results. Humans are very clever animals and cats are smart enough to learn that humans can learn a set of meowed commands!

There's a meow for 'let me out', another for 'let me in', and another for 'I'm hungry' and 'I missed you' or 'pick me up'. Remember, meows are reserved for humans; they are rarely used feline to feline. There is even a 'silent meow' which is often accompanied with the tap of a paw. It is reputed to be the most persuasive of cat pleas, reserved for the more dominant members of the household to melt the hardest hearts. (By the way, cute though it is, it's probably not a silent meow, just too high-pitched for human ears.)

Don't make the mistake of thinking that nearly every meow is a demand for food. Sometimes a single short meow just means 'hello'. Cats aren't always takers. Although genetics, cat personality and life experiences influence meowing, ultimately meows work because human responses reinforce them. If we didn't respond, cats wouldn't meow.

For example, if you find that your cat meows incessantly whenever you are on the phone and only stops when you pick her up and give her cuddles, you've taught her that behavior. The first few times she did it, you might have picked her up because she was being cute or because you wanted to end the distraction. Then you started to ignore her, because you don't always want a cat in your arms while you're on the phone, but the meowing became unbearable, so you caved in again. You alone taught your cat that she gets picked up if she meows incessantly whenever you're chatting to your hand.

Purring

When a cat nestles in your lap or lies draped across your chest and begins to purr, it feels like the ultimate compliment. For this brief moment at least, your cat would rather be nowhere else in the world. You are a feline pleasure dome, eliciting that mysterious deep rumble that signals utter contentment. However, there's more to a purr than meets the ear. Although we primarily associate it with happiness, its principal function is bonding and in early kittenhood it is vital for survival.

Kittens begin purring from a week old, even before their eyes open. They can do it without interrupting their suckling, which lets the mother know that all is well. The mother purrs to initiate feeding, like sounding a dinner gong, and also when she enters the nest, to reassure her brood. Older kittens also purr to invite adult cats to play with them and a dominant kitten will purr to reassure a more submissive littermate that he or she is not a threat. A queen on heat will purr as part of her mating display as she rolls on the ground in front of a tom and pats him coquettishly with her paw.

Cats also purr to self-soothe when they are scared or injured (which is why cats frequently purr at the vets). In fact, the frequency of the purr has been linked to ultrasonic healing. A study of 44 felids published in the Journal of the Acoustical Society of America in 2001 found that 'every felid in the study generated strong frequencies between 25 to 150Hz' which corresponds to 'vibrational/electrical frequencies used in treatment for bone growth/fractures, pain, oedema, muscle growth/strain, joint flexibility, dysprea and wounds'. The 25Hz frequency produced by domestic cats 'best promote[s] bone growth/fracture healing'.

In the wild, cats that roar (lions, tigers) do not purr, and those that purr (bobcats, mountain lions) do not roar. We still don't conclusively know how cats produce the purring sound. It may be the vibration of 'false vocal cords' next to the vocal cords; or caused by constriction of a large vein called the posterior vena cava by the cat's diaphragm; or it may be the syncopated contraction of the larynx and diaphragm.

Greeting
Sounds

The greeting body language (tail up, striding forward, looking at your face – see page 38) is often but not always accompanied by greeting sounds. The trill of welcome is often described as somewhere between a meow and a purr, which has a kind of soft plaintive urgency, that is at once needy and also seems to express pleasure. Not all cats do it though, so don't be disappointed if your cat isn't a triller; she will no doubt show you in another way that she's pleased to see you, maybe by rolling on her back.

When one cat greets another with a trill, you may hear the other cat make an acknowledgement sound, a short, inhaled purr that drops in pitch. Experiment by making this sound yourself when you get home, or match trill for trill and you may even get a bit of trilling dialogue going.

Trilling is nearly always a positive noise and is performed with the mouth closed. You may wonder why your cat doesn't just meow to say hello rather than trill. That's because your cat has developed a repertoire of noises which genuinely mean different things and are suited to different situations. You may as well ask a human why they don't grunt all the time instead of using sentences. As well as trilling upon greeting, your cat may trill to get your attention and direct it towards something of interest (such as her empty food bowl or to beg for treats).

The greeting trill is similar to the rolled meow that a mother cat uses to call her kittens to pay attention or to make a friendly approach to another cat. The mother makes a gargling sound when she arrives with prey, which differs depending on what she has caught. This is probably because different prey animals pose different degrees of risk (for example, an injured rat will be more dangerous than a bird or mouse).

HISS, SPIT AND

Growl

Cats prefer to use body language rather than sounds to communicate with each other, but when anxiety, fear or anger are high they will hiss, spit and growl. A cat hisses by opening its mouth, drawing back the upper lip and arching the tongue to expel air fast. The deep, rumbling growl noise comes from the passage of air through vocal folds.

These noises sound aggressive but they are primarily expressions of fear rather than anger. For example, your cat may growl or hiss in the presence of a dog or an unfamiliar, bigger or more dominant cat.

Cats also hiss when they are caught off guard by anything they perceive as a threat. It could be a strange object you bring into the house. The hiss is a warning that aggression will follow if you don't back off. The cat is frightened but holding its ground (prepared to fight) rather than fleeing. Many experts claim that hissing is a form of 'protective mimicry' – imitating the sound of a dangerous animal (a snake) to appear more threatening. But it is still a defensive gesture. The cat doesn't want to fight. Aggression is always the last resort and hissing is its attempt to avoid a physical confrontation.

Kittens spit at each other during play fights while they are learning boundaries and the subtleties of communication. You can use a hiss to discourage unwanted behavior. For example, if you don't want the cat jumping on the kitchen work surfaces, a quick hiss can be very effective because it is immediate and the cat already understands what it means.

FELINE NON-RECOGNITION AGGRESSION

If you have more than one cat and one of them returns from the vet, it is not uncommon for the other cats to hiss and growl. This is called 'feline non-recognition aggression'. The returning cat smells different. She smells of the vet and disinfectant and of other animals, which is much stronger than the customary smell of your house and the collective cat scent that all that rubbing helps to mingle.

Fortunately, it can be fixed quite easily. Leave the returning cat in her carrier for a few minutes while you gauge the reaction of the other cats. If trouble is brewing, take her into another room, give her a cuddle and encourage her to rub on familiar items, such as a blanket, so that she can start to smell more like home. Then introduce the other cats, one at a time, and if two of them hit it off, allow them to scent each to make the returning cat smell even more familiar.

Chatter

Some experts classify chattering as an involuntary response rather than a conscious communication noise. When a cat sees its prey but cannot reach it, a surge of adrenaline courses through its stationary body, so it's not surprising that it finds a physical outlet in chattering jaws and teeth. However, since chattering is in a cat's repertoire of noises, it merits further investigation.

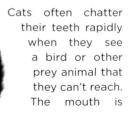

Cats often chatter their teeth rapidly when they see a bird or other prey animal that they can't reach. The mouth is slightly open, lips pulled back, the jaws open and close rapidly, often accompanied by a twittering sound. Some sources claim the cat is voicing its frustration, but while some cats may wish their tails from side to side in apparent irritation while chattering, others remain perfectly still and have no other body language that expresses annoyance. Chattering is as likely to be involuntary as a conscious expression of frustration.

Another interpretation of chattering is that the cat is mimicking its prey, enabling it to get closer. A group of scientists in the Brazilian rainforest were observing a group of pied tamarin monkeys when a wildcat arrived and started making sounds that perfectly mimicked the monkey calls. This led them to theorize that all cats may be able to copy their prey, so it certainly merits further study. Some observers report that the cat's mouth chatters in sync with the movement of the bird's beak, which may reinforce the mimicry theory.

Another possible explanation for chattering is that it's a way for a cat to alert other cats to the presence of food without alerting the prey (since it also mimics the prey). If you have several cats, you may notice that when one of them starts chattering, the others will come to the window to take a look and join in the chattering.

The chattering jaw also closely resembles the cat's 'killing bite'. Once a cat has trapped its prey, if it wants to kill the animal quickly (rather than take it home as a gift for you or for its kittens to use for hunting practice), the cat bites the back of the prey's neck and then rapidly vibrates its jaws to sever the spinal cord. This swift kill is not only efficient but also minimizes the risk of the prey injuring the cat.

WAIL AND

Yowl

There are many reasons for a cat to wail or howl and those noises aren't all fighting talk. Female cats in heat will yowl plaintively with a slight strangulation quality to attract tomcats. When two male cats are in a stand-off about to fight, the yowl (in this context called caterwauling) is the final vocal warning before the fight begins.

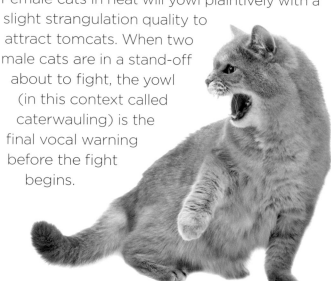

Older cats may wail because they are disoriented and suffering from sensory loss (hearing, smell, sight) or dementia. An old cat will often yowl at night because everyone is asleep, no one is paying her any attention, she feels confused, or lonely and bored, stomping restlessly around the house making 'excessive vocalization'. Other medical reasons for yowling include high blood pressure, hyperthyroidism (cat feels hungry all the time), chronic pain or a slow-growing brain tumour called a meningioma. If in doubt, see a vet.

If you've adopted an older cat that's used to being with other cats, she may walk around wailing looking for housemates that are no longer there. Or she may just wake up feeling confused and not know where she is. An older noisy cat may also have digestion issues, so it's worth discussing with your vet ways of helping her in this area.

If your cat is excessively noisy and you've ruled out medical and other reasons, go back to basics and make sure that her essential needs are being covered, such as a clean individual litter tray, clean water and food. Sometimes a noisy cat is simply trying to improve the quality of the room service.

You can also reduce night time restlessness by playing an active game with your cat before bed to wear her out and tune the radio to something soothing such as easy listening, smooth classical or talk. As a general rule, the best way to discourage unwanted behavior is to ignore it and to focus on other healthier diversions. There's no point shushing or shouting at a noisy cat because even negative attention is still attention, so you are rewarding your cat for unwanted behavior. Wait until the unwanted noise has stopped, then reward the silence with your company, a little food or play.

Beep and Burble

The 'beep' (also known as 'bip' or 'eek') is a general attention-seeking sound which many cat owners interpret as 'Err, excuse me'.

When your cat beeps and then just stares at you, she wants something and she's waiting for you to make the next move. It may be simply that she wants to jump up on your lap and beeps to alert you, then she waits for an invitation, which might be vocal, or you might be accustomed to tapping on your lap.

The burble is a peculiar combination of a purr, a meow and a growl. It's generally interpreted as an appreciative sound (despite the growl quality) and means something like 'thanks for your attention'.

Prowling his own quiet backyard or asleep by the fire, he is still only a whisker away from the wilds.

JEAN BURDEN

SEE YOU,

Feel You

BONDING THROUGH

Grooming

Cats love to groom themselves, each other and to be groomed by humans. It's important for bonding as well as health, skin, fur, circulation, creating a group smell and to relieve stress.

Kittens instinctively groom themselves from about 3 weeks old, even before they can walk. Their barbed tongues remove loose hair, stimulate new hair growth and blood supply to the skin, prevent matting and spread secretions to keep the coat waterproof. Cats also groom to control their body temperature: the evaporation of saliva produces cooling, or, when it's cold, grooming helps to keep the fur fluffy to provide maximum insulation.

Start grooming your kitten as soon as possible so that it becomes a normal part of her routine. Before weaning, the mother cleans her kittens by licking them, so you are creating a strong bond by taking over the mother's grooming role.

Long-haired cats need more regular grooming than short-haired cats to prevent little tangles from developing into big and problematic matted areas that pull on the skin and cause a lot of discomfort.

- Pick a time when the cat is relaxed and contented, maybe after feeding when she's feeling satisfied and sleepy.

- Use a fine-toothed comb for a short-haired cat or a wide-toothed comb for a long-haired cat to remove any dirt or grit that may be caught in the cat's coat. Carefully work out any knots.

- Follow up with a wire brush or a bristle brush to remove loose hair.

- You can use a toothbrush to brush around the cat's face.

- Groom for up to 10 minutes, then reward the cat with a little treat.

You'll quickly learn what your cat likes best, whether it's having her head and cheeks brushed or the base of her tail. She will usually respond favourably to rhythmical brushing or stroking because it is more predictable and she can relax knowing there will be no surprises, but also because the rhythm itself is soothing and soporific. Short-haired cats can be groomed two or three times a week, but long-haired cats need grooming every day.

THE BEST AND WORST PLACES TO

Touch

It is important for a kitten's socialization with humans that she is handled regularly during the early weeks (and beyond) so that she learns to feel safe with the humans in her life and that no part of her body is out of bounds. However, even with the best bonding and grooming sessions, she still has areas of her body that are more sensitive or are more vulnerable to touch than others. You should learn where they are and respect her sensitivities.

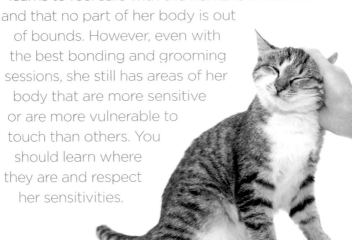

The most vulnerable area of a cat's body is the tummy, which is why she has to feel really safe and trusting to lie sprawled on her back with her tummy exposed. As indicated elsewhere in this book, that's not necessarily an invitation for you to dive in with your big ham hands to rub her tummy. Should you stroke her tummy and see her tail twitch, run for the hills. You're about to get paw swiped or even bitten and it will be your own fault – she is only exhibiting a basic defence reflex.

Many cats dislike people messing with their paw pads. Humans find the undersides of cats' paws so cute that we often can't resist touching them and revelling in their shiny perfection. However, cats have very sensitive paws with lots of nerve endings, so while it's important to regularly examine them to make sure they're clean and free from injury (cracks, cuts, abrasions, bleeding or swelling), most cats won't thank you for fussing with them. Cats literally feel the ground through their paw pads and they are very important for balance, cushioning and hunting.

Did you know that the color of your cat's paws is related to the color of her fur? Black cats have black paw pads, white cats and orange cats have pink paw pads, grey cats have grey, pink or purple paw pads and multicolored cats can have mottled paw pads.

Most cats love nothing better than to be stroked and tickled around the head and will push their heads hard into your hands as you stroke them. Other favorite spots include the area between or behind the ears and the cheeks just behind the whiskers. Avoid touching the whiskers themselves, including the ones above the eyes. If you're ever in doubt about whether your cat is enjoying the attention, just listen to the loudness of its purring.

SO WHY DOES SHE ROLL OVER ON HER
Back?

You might feel you have every right to feel disgruntled, played and exploited when your cat rolls around enticingly on her back and then bites you when you tickle her tummy. She definitely seems to want something from you. If only she wasn't so capricious and inscrutable you could figure out what it was.

Cats roll around on their back showing their bellies for a variety of reasons. Sometimes it's a simple back scratch to get the blood flowing around the back and spine. Try it yourself sometime, with your shirt off and preferably on a jute rug; it's awesome. It gives your back a fantastic massage, engages your stomach muscles as you press your back into the floor, improves flexibility and leaves you feeling relaxed and energized all at the same time. Even if you start without an itch to scratch, once the blood gets flowing in your back, the stimulation of nerves soon makes it feel as if the whole region is crying out for a giant s-c-r-a-t-c-h. Don't overdo it though or you'll end up with carpet burns – all in the name of understanding your cat.

During the early 1990s, Hilary Feldman of Cambridge University's Sub-Department of Animal Behavior, spent six months observing the phenomenon of cat rolling and in 1994 published the results in 'Domestic Cats and Passive Submission' in the journal Animal Behavior. It's common for female cats to roll when they are in heat: 'Females roll primarily in the presence of adult males, demonstrating a readiness to mate'. But Feldman also concluded that 'males roll near adult males as a form of subordinate behavior' and 'that rolling may act as passive submission and inhibits the development of overt aggression'. Feldman went on to suggest that this 'phenomenon of passive submission may have relevance for a similar behavior between pet cats and their owners'. Cats roll around to placate us and it certainly works – we find rolling cats irresistible.

One other plausible reason for rolling is that it's a way of inviting play. So even if your cat doesn't want a tummy rub, it may be the perfect time to fetch the dangle toys.

AGGRESSIVE BEHAVIOR

Between Cats

If you have several cats, introduce a new cat or a new cat arrives in your neighborhood, you can expect to witness aggressive behavior between cats, including body language and vocalizations. There are three common types of aggressive behavior between cats: territorial, inter-male and defensive aggression.

TERRITORIAL AGGRESSION

Both male and female cats are very territorial, even more so than dogs. Territorial aggression happens when a cat feels that its territory has been threatened by another cat. In the wild, territory is determined by the availability of food, not by the size of the landscape. Cats mark their territory by scratching, spraying, urine and faeces deposits and by rubbing their scent. Cats can read these markers and use the information to share territory whilst staying out of each other's way (for example, one cat might hunt in the area during the morning, another cat during the afternoon). However, when physical confrontation occurs, you will see a cat chasing away or ambushing an intruder, as well as hissing and paw swatting.

INTER-MALE AGGRESSION

Adult intact males habitually indulge in aggressive displays, and occasionally fights, with other males, either as a sexual challenge over a female in heat or to establish dominance. This usually involves ritualized body posturing (arching the back, puffing up the fur to appear bigger), stalking, stare-offs and yowling. If there is a fight, one cat will pounce and attack the neck of its opponent, who may respond by lying on his back and trying to bite and scratch the attacker's belly. They may roll around like this screaming for a few seconds, before one of the cats runs away.

DEFENSIVE AGGRESSION

Cats adopt a posture of defensive aggression when they feel that a fight is inevitable and inescapable. She crouches with legs pulled underneath the body, ears flat and facing backwards, tail tucked into the body. This is not the same as the submissive posture used by dogs, which is intended to make them appear unthreatening. At this stage, the cat has passed the point of appeasement and she's protecting her body rather than being submissive.

SIXTH

Sense

Cats and many other animals have been revered and feared over the centuries for their ability to foretell a storm, earthquake, volcano eruption or other natural disaster, and more recently for their ability to detect illness in humans. In the past, cats have been worshipped and persecuted in equal measure, not least for this mysterious sixth sense.

Today, we can at least partially explain how cats are able to predict these freak events. Before a large seismic event, modern seismographs are now able to detect foreshocks – smaller disturbances that become progressively stronger and more closely spaced leading up to the main quake. Scientists are hoping to develop this system more widely so they can offer at least a limited early warning of a few hours. Cats are very sensitive to vibrations and, through their feet and whiskers, it's highly likely that they can detect these foreshocks. They may become agitated as these vibrations become stronger and more frequent, in the same way that we know when something scary is about to happen in a horror film because of the urgent soundtrack.

A volcanic eruption is often preceded by foreshocks and the release of chemicals into the air through the ground. These would be easily detected by a cat's powerful sense of smell.

When cats predict storms, they may be relying on smell and taste as well as their sensitivity to electromagnetism. Even humans can smell a storm coming. Before the rain begins, you may notice the smell of ozone in the air, carried down from high altitudes by downdrafts. It has the chemical symbol O_3 because each molecule of ozone has one more oxygen atom than regular oxygen (O_2), which makes it smell zingy and fresh. Cats will certainly detect this change in the air. Storms also generate a lot of electrical activity, which cats will detect in their fur and whiskers. Some cats rub their ears before a storm, perhaps because changes in air pressure are affecting their sensitive inner ear.

Predicting illness in humans also relies on smell and taste. A cat called Oscar appeared in the New England Journal of Medicine in 2007 and recently found tabloid fame having predicted the deaths of dozens of people over several years at Steere House Nursing Center in Providence, Rhode Island. The author of the report, Dr David Dosa, observed: 'he only comes to the end of life patients who are near death, I think he is attracted in some capacity to them. I think he probably is responding to a pheromone or a scent'.

Feline Facial Expressions

In 1979, after decades of studying a wide variety of wild and domestic cats, German zoologist and behavioral scientist, Paul Leyhausen, published the seminal book *Cat Behavior: Predatory and Social Behavior of Domestic and Wild Cats*. Leyhausen gave a description of the facial expressions of cats with illustrations to provide a definitive guide to understanding a cat's emotional state, associated with offensive and defensive behavior, through the observation of the ears, eyes, mouth and other key features. This famous illustration remains a benchmark for feline behaviorists and cat lovers and proves that cats really do have facial expressions.

An article in the April 2017 edition of *Discover* magazine revisited Leyhausen's work and describes the illustration as a 'largely anecdotal description that can be easily misunderstood'. The article discusses how a more sophisticated 'facial action coding system has been developed for cats (CatFACS), similar to that used for objectively coding human facial expressions'. Video recordings of 29 cats in a Canadian animal shelter were analyzed and the results confirmed and extended Leyhausen's work:

'Facial actions associated with fear included blinking and half-blinking and a left head and gaze bias at lower intensities. Facial actions consistently associated with frustration included hissing, nose-licking, dropping of the jaw, the raising of the upper lip, nose wrinkling, lower lip depression, parting of the lips, mouth stretching, vocalization and showing of the tongue. Relaxed engagement appeared to be associated with a right gaze and head turn bias.'

TEN SIGNS OF
Illness

Unless your cat is very lucky, she will get ill at some point in her life. Therefore, it's worth knowing a few signs of illness and their possible causes. The following advice is only an introduction and no substitute for consulting a trained professional. If you have any concerns about the health of your kitten or cat, contact your vet immediately.

EYE DISCHARGE

Cats get crusty bits in the corner of their eyes, just like humans, and usually they are no cause for worry. However, if your cat has a persistent yellow discharge coming from her eye, she may have an allergy, infection or injury. Wipe away the gunk with a clean damp towel and if it the problem persists, visit the vet.

VOMITING

Most cats will produce hairballs at some point in their lives. The hair builds up in the cat's digestive system until it is vomited up. The occasional hairball isn't an issue and you can reduce them by daily brushing. Persistent vomiting, even of hairballs, usually requires veterinary advice. Causes include a change in diet, eating grass, food poisoning, intestinal parasites, diabetes, kidney or thyroid problems, swallowing a foreign object or inflammatory bowel disease.

SWOLLEN STOMACH

A bulging stomach could be a sign of overeating. Instead of giving your cat two meals during the day, offer several smaller ones. If that makes no difference, she may have intestinal parasites such as worms. Visit your vet for a check up and de-wormer if required.

LETHARGY

Cats and especially kittens spend a lot of time sleeping, but they are also highly active, playful and inquisitive when they are awake. You'll soon get to know what a normal level of activity is for your cat. If she appears to have lost all interest in her surroundings and just wants to sleep, contact your vet.

LOSS OF APPETITE

If your cat eats something that makes her poorly or if she is suffering from a bacterial or viral infection, she will stop eating for a few days. Often this is all that is required to allow her body to recover. While she is on the mend, you can offer her mild, easily digestible food such as boiled chicken or unseasoned boiled rice. If she still won't eat anything, see the vet.

PROBLEMS URINATING

If your cat makes several trips to the litter tray without producing any results or starts urinating in unusual places outside the litter tray, she may have a urinary tract infection or blockage. If the color of the urine is much darker than normal – deep orange, brown or red instead of the normal yellow – she may be dehydrated or have something more serious such as kidney problems.

PANTING, COUGHING, SNEEZING AND WHEEZING

When a cat pants or coughs it is usually a sign of overheating or overexertion. Take your cat somewhere cool and encourage her to stay still and calm down. Sneezing, wheezing or repeated coughing is often the sign of a respiratory tract problem or something else that requires immediate attention, so don't delay, visit the vet right away.

DIARRHOEA

Diarrhoea is commonly caused by a sudden change of diet. If you run out of cat food and offer a short-term substitute, you can expect your cat to get diarrhoea. But loose stools can be a sign of more serious problems, such as a blockage in the bowel or another part of the digestive system, dietary deficiency, intestinal parasites or even acute anxiety. If you can't pin it down to a simple change in diet or mealtime, see your vet.

WHITE GUMS

Your cat's gums should be light pink. If you notice that they are white, rush her to the vet immediately as this is a sure sign of anaemia, a blood disorder that requires urgent medical treatment.

SIGNS OF POISONING

If your cat is drooling, has diarrhoea and lethargy, loss of appetite or pale or yellowish gums, these could be the early effects of poisoning. The symptoms progress with excessive thirst or urination and tell-tale nervousness, muscle twitching or seizures and then coma. As soon as you suspect that your cat has ingested poison, it is imperative that you get treatment as quickly as possible. The vet will need to administer an emetic to make the cat vomit to minimize the internal damage and then sedate her to control life-threatening seizures if the symptoms are well advanced.

I put my hand on the cat's chest and felt his heart beating. The pulse was faint and fast, but his heart, like mine, was ticking off the time allotted to his small body with all the restless earnestness of my own.

HARUKI MURAKAMI

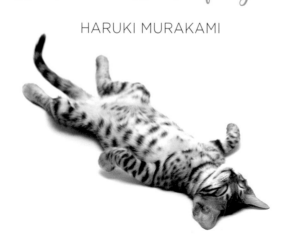

GROWING

Together

TEACHING
Vocabulary

Cats can learn vocabulary – about 25 to 35 words. This is much lower than the average dog, which can learn about 165 words and many more with specialist training. Chaser the border collie has a vocabulary of over 1,000 words – the largest of any dog on the planet and way beyond anything a cat could achieve. However, cats have many more vocalizations than dogs and, as we have seen throughout this book, there are many ways to communicate with a cat beyond human-centric vocabulary.

Dogs may know more words, but they can only produce about 15 different sounds. Cats may only understand 35 words, but they can produce about 100 different vocalizations. Cats make more effort to communicate, whereas it could be said that dogs are better listeners.

Cats, like dogs, find it easier to understand concrete words that relate to things, rather than abstract concepts. Your cat will respond better to words like 'tuna' or 'treat' rather than 'I love you' where all she will understand is the soothing tone and not attach any further meaning to it.

Name each of your cat's toys so that she can associate a concrete word with objects that hold her attention as much as 'dinner'. If you teach her a word like 'hungry' you may think she is responding to an abstract concept, but really she will learn to associate the word with every time you take a tin of cat food out of the kitchen cupboard. She'll know it relates to food and she may meow loudly in response to tell you that she's hungry, but that's not the same thing as responding to an abstract concept.

If you are keen to expand your cat's vocabulary, just remember not to get too hung up on words. Sometimes it will do you good to talk less and pay attention to the many other ways your cat communicates with you. The good news is that a new study by Japanese researchers at the University of Tokyo, published in the journal Animal Cognition, has revealed that cats do pay attention when they are spoken to. 'How words are spoken is really important,' says feline behaviorist Marilyn Krieger. 'Cats are very sensitive and can feel safe or feel threatened by the tone of voice and the loudness. Cats are more apt to respond and socialize with their people when spoken to in a soft and calm voice'.

Consistency
is Key

When dealing with any pet, especially cats, consistency is key for communication, but it is also the basis for providing your cat with a familiar routine so that she can feel happy and secure. Cats become nervous and anxious when there are too many changes to their routine. This soon translates into physical expressions: chewing, biting, scratching, not using the litter box and excessive grooming.

Your entire day doesn't have to be regimented down to the minute, but if you can manage to do feeding, playing, grooming and other regular activities at roughly the same time every day, your cat can use these signposts to structure her day. Imagine if you spent every day of your life not knowing when you were going to eat, sleep, take a shower or see your friends. All animals need some routine, otherwise they feel out of control. Establish these routines early on and they won't become a battleground later (e.g. reluctant grooming sessions).

Most people have fairly well-structured days, but if you suddenly experience a big change, such as introducing a new family member or pet, or going to work and leaving the house all day rather than staying at home, this will inevitably impact on your cat.

Routine means consistency: be consistent in your intent and expression. For example, if you're busy and you don't have time to pet or play with her, say in a firm tone, 'later' and turn your body away from her. Don't send mixed messages by stroking her and tickling her chin because you feel guilty. This just confuses the cat and it's little wonder she comes back to disturb you eight more times.

Use a commanding tone (deep, loud and firm but not shouting) when she is doing something that you consider wrong and that you want her to stop. She may look impossibly cute or funny while she is misbehaving, but don't laugh or you'll send mixed messages again. If you want your cat to respect boundaries in your house, then you have to be consistent.

You can even make a quick and sharp hiss or spit sound to say 'no'. She will understand this instinctively because it is part of the corrective cat language between mother and kitten.

TRAINING FOR

Tricks

As we have seen on page 116, cats can learn a limited vocabulary. It is also possible to train cats to respond to certain words and to do tricks, although it's not as easy as training a dog. Cats, despite their reputation as aloof loners, are perfectly trainable. They can even be trained to compete in agility tournaments. Remember, cats respond to positive reinforcement, not negative punishment.

Dr Mikel Maria Delgado studies human-pet behavior, specifically cat behavior, and is co-author of the book Total Cat Mojo with pet behaviorist and star of the hit television show My Cat From Hell, Jackson Galaxy. She says: 'it's sadly easy to teach a cat to sit. When you pick things that they kind of do anyway, it only takes a few minutes'. You can train cats to respond to specific words like 'sit' in much the same way you'd teach a dog – with repetition and rewards. However, food isn't always the best reward for cat training. A piece of kibble from her regular cat food just won't do. If you're going to use food treats, you'd better make sure they're your cat's absolute favorites – diced chicken, lumps of tuna, whatever you know sends her wild.

You might get better results with petting or playtime with a favorite toy than with food. Cats have a much shorter attention span than dogs, so you need to catch them when they are receptive and keep training sessions very short – just a few minutes.

Once your cat has mastered a trick, you'll still have to repeat the routine again the next day and keep revisiting it regularly, otherwise she will quickly forget what she has learned.

Above all, if you really want to teach your cat tricks, make sure it's fun for both of you and don't expect your cat to behave like a dog. Jackson Galaxy warns that 'most of the problems that I encounter are people looking at cats through dog colored glasses, they're just expecting cats to respond like dogs, to seek approval like dogs, it's not how they work. They didn't ride the same train as dogs did throughout history and so it's not fair to compare them'.

HOW TO MASSAGE
Your Cat

After smell, touch is the next best way to bond with your cat. The great thing about massage is that it benefits both the receiver and the giver. Cats love to be stroked and petted so massage is a totally natural extension of this healthy and pleasurable activity that you already enjoy. However, properly performed, massage will actually benefit your cat's health and wellbeing as well as deepen your special bond.

1. Choose a time when your cat is already relaxed and conducive to being handled. If at any time she shows her displeasure or wants to leave, don't keep her against her will. Have another try later.

2. The most passive massage technique involves simply placing your hands palms down onto an area of the body and just allowing the warmth of your hands to soothe and nurture as you apply very gentle pressure.

3. Move on to the basic stroke known as effleurage (flow or glide). Starting behind the ears and using your whole hand, make a series of long, flowing, gentle strokes,

which move down the length of your cat's back to her tail, applying gentle pressure on either side of her spine. Be very gentle at first so that it feels just like a firmer than usual stroke. If your cat is happy, you can apply firmer pressure, but be very careful as you are much stronger and bigger than her. Also apply light effleurage strokes along the limbs, starting from the body and working towards the paw.

4. Another basic technique is called petrissage, which is a gentle rhythmical kneading action on the muscle areas, using both hands, applying gentle pressure with one hand while you release it with the other.

The health benefits of massage include:

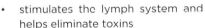

- discovering unknown lumps, bumps and injuries

- relieving joint and muscle pain and aches (yes, your cat does get them)

- detecting ticks and other parasites

- improves circulation and blood flow to the muscles, skin and major organs

- stimulates the lymph system and helps eliminate toxins

- improves the quality of the coat

- produces deep relaxation (surely your cat doesn't need any help with that, does she?).

TWENTY FACTS EVERY CAT LOVER

Should Know

1. All cats are in the Felidae family, of which there are two living subfamilies: Pantherinae (which includes jaguars, lions, leopards and tigers) and Felinae (which includes cougars, cheetahs, lynxes, ocelots and domestic cats). There was a third – now extinct – subfamily called Machairodontinae, which included the smilodon (the saber-toothed tiger which died out about 12,000 years ago).

2. The most recent common ancestor of all three subfamilies was a prehistoric cat called Pseudaelurus that lived in Eurasia and North America about 20 million years ago, had short legs and looked like a weasel. It died out about 8 million years ago.

3. Scientists used to think that cats were first domesticated by the Egyptians about 4,000 years ago, but new evidence has pushed this back to 10,000 years ago and to parts of what is now Cyprus. Every breed of household cat alive today originates from just five lineages which lived alongside Neolithic humans in the Fertile Crescent, stretching from the eastern Mediterranean to the Persian Gulf and irrigated by the waters of the Nile, Jordan, Tigris and Euphrates.

4. During the time of the Spanish Inquisition, Pope Innocent VIII condemned cats as evil and thousands were tortured and burned. This led to an explosion of the rat population that was once thought to have contributed to the spread of the Black Death. However, recent research has shown that it was largely spread by human fleas and body lice.

5. A cat's brain is biologically more similar to a human brain than it is to a dog's. Cats and humans have very similar regions in the brain responsible for emotions.

6. Most kittens are born with bright blue eyes, but many change color by adulthood.

7. Unlike humans, cats can survive by drinking sea water because their kidneys are able to filter out the salt without becoming fatally damaged.

8. All mammals, except for members of the Felidae family, can taste sweetness.

9. The furry tufts on the inside of cats' ears are called 'ear furnishings'.

10. Isaac Newton is credited with being an early adopter of the cat flap after his own cat, Spithead, kept opening the door of his laboratory and spoiling his experiments. Newton paid a carpenter to cut two holes in the door (a large one for the cat and another smaller one for her kittens) and then he hung a black velvet cloth over the holes to keep out the light.

11. A group of cats is called a clowder; a group of kittens is called a kindle.

12. A cat has five toes on his front paws and four on the back, unless he's a polydactyl cat (a cat born with a congenital anomaly that means he has more than the usual number of toes).

13. When a domestic cat died in ancient Egypt, family members would shave off their eyebrows in mourning.

14. Cats walk like camels, giraffes and brown bears: they move both legs on one side, then move both legs on the other side. No other mammals walk like this. This was an evolutionary advantage for these animals when careful and quiet walking was important for survival.

15. Cats typically sleep for 12 to 16 hours a day and can spend up to a third of their waking hours grooming.

16. Many cats are lactose intolerant and so they shouldn't be offered cow's milk or cream.

17. Catnip (Nepeta cataria) produces an effect similar to LSD or marijuana in cats. The active ingredient nepetalactone ($C_{10}H_{14}O_2$) will make most cats crazy for about 15 minutes, after which a second sniff will have no effect until several hours have passed.

18. Cats really dislike citrus scents, but some cats love the smell of chlorine (and love sniffing their owner's hair after they've been swimming).

19. Kittens in the same litter can have more than one father. A female cat releases several eggs over the few days that she's in heat.

20. A female cat gestates for about 58-65 days before giving birth.

When a cat adopts you there is nothing to be done about it except to put up with it until the wind changes!

TS ELIOT